Think Outside the Box:
The Most Trite, Generic, Hokey, Overused, Cliched or Unmotivating Motivational Slogans

by Jim Tompkins

Tompkins Press
Raleigh, North Carolina

Library of Congress Cataloging-in-Publication Data

Tompkins, Jim
    Think outside the box: the most trite, generic, hokey, overused, cliched or unmotivating motivational slogans / Jim Tompkins. - 1 st. ed.

    LCCN: 2001 126007
    ISBN: 1-930426-02-X

> "I have never thought that one picture
> is worth a thousand words,
> but it is certainly true that one slogan
> can blot out a thousand thoughts."
>
> *-Sydney J. Harris*

Few forms of expression oversimplify thoughts more than slogans. Yet, some people and some organizations will insist that there is always a time and place for slogans. In fact, many corporate leaders rely on slogans to energize their organizations. This is unfortunate because often the slogans do not accomplish their objectives or if they do they have a short shelf life. Even when slogans have a short-term value, however, their overall value is still suspect because as a slogan nears the end of its shelf life, it can lead to wry jokes, cynicism, and even bitterness.

My 25 years of consulting to some of the world's top organizations have taught me that slogans have an allure that is shallow. Despite the repeated failures of glitzy phrases as quick fixes, slogans continue to proliferate as motivational mechanisms. Many believe slogans can rally the troops and therefore provide an easy solution. But even the freshest, most original slogans quickly become stale objects of derision.

As a strong believer in the science of business and, therefore, a strong adversary of quick fixes, easy solutions, and empty words, I have always had a fascination with slogans and organizations that perpetuate them. To better understand the allure of slogans and provide some fun reading, my staff and I conducted a contest to identify "The Most Trite, Generic, Hokey, Overused, Cliched, or Unmotivating Motivational Slogan." Contestants inundated us with entries by fax, e-mail, and the Web. People scrawled slogans on index cards and stuffed them in envelopes. Many who sent in slogans also had retorts for the slogans. They wrote on company letterhead with the circumstances of the offense acutely detailed. Some entrants sent actual memos introducing these slogans, and some even offered to collect corroborating evidence if only we would expose their company's insensitive tactics.

The abundant responses confirmed that slogans are very much alive, but not well. The contest also revealed a negative backlash. Instead of motivating people or organizations, slogans often stir up or intensify hostility. The more contest responses I read the more convinced I became that there was a real lesson to be gained by sharing the submitted slogans. After all, one of the best ways to learn is by reflecting on mistakes. In this case, I recommend reflecting on the mistakes made by others in their pursuit of easy solutions via slogans.

I have organized the contest responses around eight general themes that have concerned organizations since the beginning of the Industrial Revolution:

▶

1. Problem solving
2. Attitudes and morale
3. Customer focus
4. Organizational excellence
5. Motivation and leadership
6. Teamwork
7. Dealing with change
8. Employee humor.

Each of these themes is the subject of a chapter with a final chapter that addresses the last word on "thinking outside the box." Throughout I have added my thoughts on the slogans to help stimulate your thoughts and learning. I strongly encourage organizations to stop trying to substitute slogans for leadership and encourage you to enjoy this little book and learn from the mistakes of others.

For their commitment to making this book a reality, I'd like to thank Kami Spangenberg, Brian Geis, and Brenda Jernigan. Pam King, Tonya Loggains, Scheryl Schonauer, Myra Schwartz, Tarsha Bracey, and Meg House provided invaluable design work, proofing, comments, and production assistance. As always, it is a pleasure to work with these publications professionals at Tompkins.

Chapter 1
Think outside the box

Problem Solving

"Think outside the box" means, *"Go beyond the limits of conventional wisdom to find solutions."* There is merit in the thought, but not in the expression. In this chapter are other lackluster recommendations for solving problems and creating ideas. As you will see, these slogans and cliches tell us to solve problems, but they don't tell us how.

Don't just solve problems, create opportunities!

Every problem is an opportunity.

It's not a problem—it's an opportunity.

If you don't know what you're doing, don't do anything.

If you think you can't, you won't. If you think you can, you will.

If you're not living on the edge, you're taking up too much room.

If you're not part of the solution, you're part of the problem.

There is an island of opportunity in the middle of every difficulty.

"

The currently popular phrase 'outside the box,' fits the contest criteria perfectly. It pre-supposes in the most denigrating way that employees are unimaginative, uncreative, and stupid. The only clue to the faintest possibility of it being true is that the person works for someone who uses such a phrase.

-*Linda*

"

To find the solution to your problem, you have got to peel away the layers of that onion. In reality, this means, 'Though I sound like a deep thinker, I have no clue how to solve your problem.'

–Barbara

THINKING

"The mind is like an umbrella— only working when it's open."

I would say the mind, like an umbrella, works best when it's open. Both will still work when they're closed. A closed umbrella makes an effective club, and a closed mind, unfortunately, can generate destructive ideas. Cliches on thinking in the workplace abound.

Only those who see the invisible can do the impossible.

The difficult we do right away, the impossible takes a little longer.

Some students drink at the fountain of knowledge. Others just gargle.

Thinking is the hardest work there is, which is probably why so few people engage in it.

You can do anything you put your mind to.

This slogan is constantly being used, particularly by athletes doing community service, and just really doesn't make a whole lot of sense when you think about it. I'm all for trying to instill confidence and motivation, but this seems especially ironic coming from a seven-foot-tall NBA power forward. You mean, if I put my mind to it, I could dunk just like you?

-Erik

*J*ust to show that, indeed, great words can be trivialized if great leadership doesn't follow, we received a quote written by one of the great individualists of our time, Ralph Waldo Emerson:

"What lies behind us
and what lies before us
are tiny matters compared
to what lies within us."

Think.

Great minds think alike.

There are no shortcuts, only costly detours.

Of course there are shortcuts. Our challenge is to identify them and not get caught up in short-term optimism.

IDEAS

Corporations and managers have various quick cliches on ideas:

Your bright ideas help give us all a brighter future.

Let's run that idea up the flagpole and see who salutes.

The sun never sets on bright ideas.

You can send a message around the world in 1/7 of a second; yet it may take several years to move a simple idea through a 1/4 inch of human skull.

There is no such thing as a bad idea.

How about the Edsel? Or the "new" Coke? Perhaps you should not identify an idea as bad to its originator, but to say there are no bad ideas is crazy. Bad ideas can be costly and even ruinous.

I am a federal civil service employee. As you may know, we workers are faced with 'bidding' for our very jobs against private contractors. To start, private contractors no longer have to pay union scale wages for all their employees that work on federal property. If they only get awarded the job and hire subcontractors, the subcontractor controls the wages and working conditions of most of those that actually perform the work. Since most of these workers are hired as part-time, there are no benefits paid or allotted for. We federal employees are faced with stringent safety and EPA regulations that the contractor can freely ignore. In most contracts with the federal government, if a contractor is fined for any infringement of regulations, the contractor merely bills the government as unforeseen ▶

costs and recoups their fines. Our management then offers what we, the workers, can offer as a bid to the program. The workers are kept in the dark and not allowed input because we 'must do more with less and work smarter!' Historically, only the smartest of the current management is left as a 'liaison' when the civil service system loses. One morning there appeared a banner on our building in our work area. Printed in large black letters on a white background, it said 'Your bright ideas help give us all a brighter future.' Should you care to e-mail me a good snail mail address, I'll cut the banner down and mail it to you.   *-Name Withheld*

  15

Chapter 2

If you are not fired with enthusiasm, you will be fired... with enthusiasm!

Attitudes and Morale

Everyone agrees that attitude is important for achieving success. But how do we build good attitudes? Although the following slogans testify that good attitudes are essential, they do not contribute to creating a good attitude.

Attitude is a little thing that makes a big difference.

Attitude is the mind's paintbrush. It can color any situation.

Each employee is the face of the company.

To all employees: Please check your bad attitudes at the door.

Your attitude determines your altitude.

Be enthusiastic. Think you can.

Winners never quit. Quitters never win.

Great service starts with a good attitude.

Your attitude is your business!

Work smarter, not harder.

Never let them rest until your good is better and your better is best.

The best steam to have is self-esteem.

Happy employees are productive employees.

'Work smarter, not harder' is a great thing to be told, especially after being left after a downsizing with a triple-sized workload. Suddenly, after 15 years with a company, overtime is not allowed and you're not very bright if you can't fit a 12-hour workday into eight hours! *-Margaret*

MORALE BOOSTERS?

A popular directive in organizations is "Create your own destiny." It is meant to inspire good work, but in reality, it is an example of how morale boosting slogans rarely do boost morale. Telling someone that he or she creates his or her own destiny also absolves an organization of all blame if that destiny is the unemployment line. It's like saying, "This is all your fault."

Many morale boosters are questionable.

When the going gets tough, the tough get going.
This is attributed as a World War I slogan aimed at inducing the troops to jump out of the trenches and into the machine gun fire, so that arms companies could get rich. *-James*

  The Most Trite, Generic, Hokey, Overused, Cliched or Unmotivating Motivational Slogans •

Be kind to all, be intimate with few, and may the few be well-chosen.

Don't worry—be happy.

Tough times don't last; tough people do.

Believe it to achieve it.

  25

"

All you need is a little elbow grease.
My husband is the originator of this statement. It is used by him
to mean your elbow grease, not his!   *-Gloria*

"

Empower your employees.

The sky's the limit!

To be a winner, all you need is to give all you have.

You can make a difference.

These represent an optimistic view, it's true. However, they do little to boost morale because they don't have any substance. One of the ways to be certain that employees understand and appreciate the vision and the mission of where the company is going is to develop a Model of Success (MOS). An MOS improves employee morale—in a study done by Kouzes and Posner, asking people to explain when people performed at their best, it was found that when a Model of Success was effectively communicated, significantly higher levels of job satisfaction, commitment, loyalty, esprit de corps, clarity about organizational values, pride in the organization, organizational productivity, and encouragement to be productive all resulted. For more information on the Model of Success go on-line to www.tompkinsinc.com/think. What else can be done to improve employee morale? Our contest entries presented some more ideas.

THE BEATINGS WILL CONTINUE ...

"*The beatings will continue until morale improves*" is presented in jest, but underneath it is a serious view of incentives. No matter how many positive slogans are posted around an organization, most employees regard them with contempt—if they regard them at all.

A counterculture of negative slogans that address morale has also developed from these so-called "attitude adjustment" slogans. Some contest entries contained threats or veiled threats.

Do it like your life depends on it, because it just may.

Get with the program.

Hitting your stride today beats pounding the pavement tomorrow.

All whining must be in writing.

Your work around here is truly appreciated... by our competitors.

If you can't do it, your successor will.

If you can't stand the heat, get out of the kitchen.

Just be glad you HAVE a job.

Justify your paycheck every day.

If you give your all, the company will not fail.

No one is indispensable.

If you're not happy working 16-hour days,
the door swings both ways.

At my company, my boss had a favorite saying for those of us in Sales that he repeated often to help us get out there and sell. To motivate us, he found the perfect illustration: a picture of the inside of a Roman Ship. It was a fierce picture of chained, sweating, beaten men rowing under the leadership of a mean looking guy with a whip and he had written his favorite slogan: 'Row well and live.'   *-Marianne*

33

Telling employees that the company will fail unless they give it their all and that working 16-hour days is the norm misses an important point. Working hard is insufficient for you or your company to be successful. Also, overworking employees only results in tired employees. They will make mistakes, their analyses may be erroneous, and their confidence will wane. The success of an organization hinges on having alert employees, feeling good about their contribution while doing a great job.

"

Genius is 10 percent inspiration and 90 percent perspiration.
Who needs an office full of sweaty workers?   *-Mike*

"

"

As an advertising copywriter, I write slogans for a living. To my horror and amusement, I've seen how some stupid slogans can gain a foothold in an organization, take on a life of their own, and derail meaningful efforts to run a company. Here are some of my least favorite words, slogans, and phrases that are wildly overused in business: redefine (the organization; inside-out and outside-in labels an idea as the benefactor, the company, or the customer); if you will; aspirational; empower; leverage; dovetail; resonate (an idea resonates with a particular audience, i.e., rings true); interface (people do this instead of meet); tangibles (now describes things that, to my thinking, are completely intangible); the customer relationship; the customer experience; run it up the flagpole (and see who salutes); play the devil's advocate; synergistic; validate (instead of test); the future is before us; and automotive investment counselor (car salesman).   *-Shep*

"

Chapter 3
The customer is always right!

Customer Satisfaction

*M*any companies inflict their worst slogans on the very people they want to help–their customers. "The customer is always right," is just one of many trite, overused slogans.

Customers are never an inconvenience.

Our customers are the only thing keeping us in business.

Customers don't talk to the company, they talk to you!

Don't ever assume your clients know how important they are.

Your patronage is important to us.

This is a recorded message at numerous companies after the listener has waited 15 to 20 minutes to speak to a live person. *-George*

Blow away the customer!

What exactly does it mean? If we blow them away, then we won't have them anymore, will we? I see visions of customers flying through the air . . . no, I won't even go near that one! *-Rahul*

If we don't take care of the customer, somebody else will.

Our customers' interests come first.

People are our business, our only business.

The purpose of our business is to create and keep customers.

Makin' sales, havin' fun, every customer is number 1!

In truth, the customer is right about as often as we are. We need to help customers when they are not right. But we cannot accept their opinions just because they are our customers. Customers do not want you to pacify them, they want and expect fulfillment of their needs. This is our responsibility.

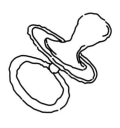

CUSTOMER SERVICE OR CUSTOMER SATISFACTION?

These concepts are blurred in the workplace and in the slogans we received.

Don't sell your products or services anymore. Instead, help the customers buy them!

We build customers for life!

Service with a smile!

Customer Service is not a department, it's an attitude.

"

We're No. 2!
Upon seeing this proclamation, a customer is supposed to ask, 'Who's No. 1?' The reply: 'You are!'   *-Bob*

"

This slogan presents too strong a temptation for the customer to simply agree that we're No. 2 and walk away.

People serving people.

Customer service is our business.

Friendly customer service.

Fast, courteous service.

Satisfaction guaranteed!

Service is satisfaction.

Not hardly. More important than customer service, which is something organizations do, is Customer Satisfaction, which is how the customer views what organizations do. Meeting or exceeding a customer's expectations will produce Customer Satisfaction.

We must be a customer-oriented company.

This slogan is useless. It implies that without direction, we would be an anti-customer company. *-Sadonna*

The Most Trite, Generic, Hokey, Overused, Cliched or Unmotivating Motivational Slogans •

Chapter 4

PRIDE =
Professional Responsibility in Delivering Excellence

Organizational Excellence

47

"Excellence" and *"excellent"* are popular words today–from teens crying *"Excellent!"* when they're pleased, to companies striving for organizational excellence. Numerous slogans promise excellence or the means to achieve it in short, choppy sound-bytes.

Go the extra mile—win "on the spot" awards!

Expect excellence.

Expect the best and you'll get the best.

Good workers make good products. Good products make good business. Good business makes good profits. To make good profits, we need good workers.

Never, never quit.

It's a double negative. Does it mean I should never, never quit?
Someone must have misspelled 'ever,' as in 'never ever quit.'
Anyway, I took the advice and quit for a better job.

-Carlos

  The Most Trite, Generic, Hokey, Overused, Cliched or Unmotivating Motivational Slogans •

Don't ever let anyone tell you that you are no good. Show everyone how good you are!

Be the best that you can be.

There are a thousand reasons for failure, but not a single excuse.

We are what we repeatedly do. Excellence is not an act but a habit.

Saying that we are what we repeatedly do glorifies habits and can be used to justify not changing or improving an operation. A good counter to this is another slogan: "If you continue to do the same thing you have always done, you will continue to get the same thing you've always gotten." And even this is not true. It is only true if everything else (not just what you do) stays the same. Today, the situation is even more challenging. When your environment changes (and it does rapidly), doing what you've always done will probably result in a future even worse than the past. To do what you've always done will not result in excellence, but in mediocrity. And, although excellence isn't an act, it also isn't really a habit. Excellence is really continuous, continuous improvement.

QUALITY

How many times have you seen posters that begin with "Our new quality policy is..." Quality is as pervasive as excellence in corporate slogans.

Quality–it's a word we like to use.

Quality is free.

Quality is presence of value and not absence of mistake.

Our company is like a book. The number of pages is determined by corporate headquarters, but the quality of the chapters is determined by each division.

Quality begins with Q.

Programs don't make quality products, people make quality products.

The memory of bad quality lasts longer than the shock of high prices.

Quality is Job One.

This last slogan, of course, is a registered trademark of Ford Motor Company. Notice the clear, direct message—no smoke and mirrors, just a solid goal. It is a good slogan. But you can be sure that Ford Motor Company relies on quality recruitment, training, and retention programs to make sure quality really is Job One, not just a slogan. Like excellence, however, quality cannot be accomplished with slogans or posters. It takes continuous, continuous improvement. (Have I mentioned that before?)

DO IT RIGHT

Slogans that emphasize excellence and quality are commonly accompanied by those that base the achievement of excellence and quality on planning, along with doing things well and correctly.

People don't plan to fail, they fail to plan.

Plan your work and work your plan.

We strive to meet our customers' expectations and needs at all times by doing it right the first time.

This phrase is on a banner in the production area where my husband works. The funny thing about it is on the adjacent wall is a bulletin board that gives monthly production statuses, which includes the number of remakes. Most of the production personnel think it's a joke.   *-Stacy*

A poor plan is better than no plan at all.

Any job worth doing is worth doing well.

It doesn't take a lot of time to do things right.

Do what you are doing very well.

Do it right the first time.

Whether the job is big or small, do it right or not at all.

Know what you have to do, set a time to complete it, then do it right.

Variations of this slogan express the frustrations of those told to do things right:

If you don't have time to do it right, when will you find time to correct it?

Why is there always enough time to do it over but never enough time to do it right the first time?

My all-time favorite worst motivational slogan is 'Do it right the first time.' If you'd give me the time, tools, and training, I would! And so would everybody else! Of course, we all learn by our mistakes, but they can be so costly.   *-Cynthia*

Organizations can prevent these frustrations if they take a Total Operations perspective of what they do. If an action is examined from the perspective of the total organization, from the warehousing, logistics, manufacturing, quality, maintenance, and organizational excellence perspectives, the chances of having to do it the second time to get it right are greatly diminished. Total Operations involves the internal collaboration of teams and the external collaboration of partners to produce continuous improvement throughout organizations. If you've read my book, **No Boundaries: Moving Beyond Supply Chain Management,** *you've seen how the Total Operations process can enhance your company's and your supply chain's success.*

Chapter 5

We can't spell success without U.

Motivation and Leadership

The secrets to success and how to make it happen were among the topics most addressed by the contestants' slogans.

Let's make it happen.

Communication is the secret to success. Pass it on.

Hard work is the key to success.

Every obstacle is a stepping stone to your success.

64

Our valued customers are the key to our success.

The key to success is ownership and passion.

Success isn't what you know, but who you know...and who you are related to.

Success makes winners.

"

'Let's make it happen' has to be the most generic phrase ever spoken. Just exactly what are we making happen? This phrase is never preceded by a set of instructions that we can then go forth and 'make happen.' For two and a half years, I worked for a company whose sales team stole this phrase from upper management and turned it into the most cheesy phrase in history. When greeting one another, 'Let's make it happen.' When passing one another, 'Let's make it happen.' This was entirely out of fun, of course; none of us was serious. Even to this day, when I am joking with someone and carrying something too far, 'Let's make it happen' will slip out and it still gets laughs.   *-John*

"

Put the U in Success!

Success is a journey, not a destination.

The journey to success starts with you.
Success makes winners.

Nothing succeeds like success.

Success is the act of getting up one more
time before getting knocked down again.

Keep your nose to the grindstone, and you will succeed.

Anything that hints toward pain or bleeding wouldn't motivate me to do anything except keep a good distance between my nose and the grindstone.
-Lori

The Most Trite, Generic, Hokey, Overused, Cliched or Unmotivating Motivational Slogans •

The reality is that success is not easy, and success is certainly not achieved through slogans. Many contestants also sent in variations on the "If at first you don't succeed..." theme.

If at first you don't succeed, try, try again.

If at first you don't succeed, to hell with it.

If at first you don't succeed, then you are running about average.

If at first you don't succeed, lower your standards.

If at first you don't succeed, redefine success.

If at first you don't succeed, try again, then give up. No sense in making a fool of yourself.

If at first you don't succeed, you're doing it wrong.

If you don't succeed after the tenth time, take a deep breath, throw up your arms, and walk away.

Most inventions would not have been invented, and most great businesses would not have become great, if people threw up their arms and walked away. Persistence is required to achieve anything worthwhile. So, if at first you don't succeed, then you are on a learning curve, and you have the opportunity to do better the next time. Even if you do succeed, that doesn't mean that you can rest on your laurels. Success demands continuous improvement. When you fail you have two choices—to beat your head against the wall or to improve. If you beat your head against the wall, you get a headache. If you take failure as an opportunity to reflect, learn, and grow based on the experience, you get better.

Why is this? Because each success leads us to the next level where we encounter more challenges. If we bask in our success and do not prepare to meet new challenges, we will fail. You may be familiar with my discussion of the cycle of peak-to-valley from my book, **Revolution: Take Charge Strategies for Business Success.** *What we want to do in our lives and our companies is move Peak-to-Peak—to succeed, face the new challenges, and succeed again. Organizations must embrace four shifts to go Peak-to-Peak:*

- *From individuals to teams*
- *From customer service to partnerships*
- *From traditional compensation to performance-based rewards and recognition*
- *From management to leadership.*

Let's look at what some of our slogans have to say about leadership.

LEADERSHIP

Success and the Peak-to-Peak experience is not possible without the right kind of leadership.

Natural leadership is defined by the "followership."

You can't be on top if you're in over your head.

He's a born leader.

You don't have to have a title to be a leader.

  73

Remember, the lead dog always has the best view.

If you ain't the lead dog, the scenery never changes.

It is true, to be a leader, you don't need a title–but it is also true that to be a leader you do need more than a slogan. Be sure you don't miss your opportunity to lead when others are depending on you. Be sure that you don't miss the opportunity to lead by relying on slogans. Leadership demands substance. Substantial collective leadership is essential to organizational growth. There is a leader within all of us.

At Tompkins Associates, we recognized the need for substantial collective leadership and created an Inspirational Leadership process. This group, which grows regularly, is involved in classes, retreats, and frequent communication. Each Inspirational Leader (IL) is at a different stage of the leadership process and contributes individual perspectives to the experience. Some may be in official leadership positions at Tompkins and may have been for many years, some may have held leadership positions outside of work, while others might just be discovering their leader within. ILs are encouraged to look inward to identify ways that they can make more of an impact. The common thread is the realization that everyone can and should take the initiative to move the company forward. Inspirational Leadership synthesizes the leadership of everyone to create a force that has limitless boundaries. Look for the inspirational leaders in your organization, not the inspirational mantras, to make a difference.

The Most Trite, Generic, Hokey, Overused, Cliched or Unmotivating Motivational Slogans •

Chapter 6

TEAM:
Together Everyone Achieves More

Team Work

Teaming is another favorite organizational slogan subject. Teaming slogans abound in cubicles, on corporate walls, and in employee training programs.

Be a team player.

We're all part of the same team.

One weak link is all it takes.

Team work is good work.

TEAMWORK: Together Everyone Achieves More with Organization, Recognition, and Knowledge.

There is no I in TEAM.

The nice thing about teams is that you always have someone on your side.

None of us is as smart as all of us.

Two heads are better than one.

"There is no I in team, but there is in FOOD CHAIN."
My new boss is a recent graduate from the St. Mary's School of Biz, or is that Buzz? Well, at any rate, he came in, removed all the old posters, and told us that crap doesn't work. Duh! So, from now on, it's top down management, only he likes to call it the 'FOOD CHAIN.'
                                                                          -Kim

The Most Trite, Generic, Hokey, Overused, Cliched or Unmotivating Motivational Slogans •

Together we can do anything.

Together we work better.

Together we're making a difference.

Together we can make it work.

Working together works.

My former workplace... started a 'team building' push when it became popular and adopted the slogan 'None of us is as smart as all of us.' This was plastered all around the workplace on cheap, 8.5 x 11-inch Xeroxed posters. However, after the posters were up about a week, some unmotivated individual used an X-acto knife and a little glue to modify one of the posters. He or she cut the N off NONE, the S off of the first AS and cut away the ALL OF US. Then the S from the first AS was added to the second AS, resulting in a poster that read, 'One of us is a smart ass.'

-Stan

Think teamwork.

A team that works together grows together!

You are not my staff. A staff is an infection. You are my team!

We're all in this together.
Ha! More often than not, [this is] offered by a boss who 'feels' for his or her underlings crunched under his or her heel in a compa-ny downsizing. *-Kolette*

  The Most Trite, Generic, Hokey, Overused, Cliched or Unmotivating Motivational Slogans •

We're all important pieces of the puzzle.

This one is as old as the hills. I am a veteran of a school corpora-
tion—truly a Dilbert world. In August, each of the librarians is
given a piece of a cardboard puzzle with the admonition that
each is a part of the final product or some such dreck. We were
further admonished to be sure and put the puzzle piece in a place
where we could see it every day and be reminded of this 'idea.'
Accompanied by giggles, tee-hees, etc. My puzzle piece went
directly in the you-know-what.   *-Name Withheld*

Many people use "team," "teaming," "teamwork," and similar words informally to mean "working together." Since people have been on various teams throughout their lives, they tend to think that teaming is a natural process that requires no special thought or effort. Many organizations have become disillusioned with teams because of misunderstandings and misapplications of teaming, or an organization's belief that a few posters with slogans praising teamwork will create a teaming atmosphere.

*Teaming is an art and a science. Teams require a special blending of purpose, personnel, timing, and trust to succeed. No slogan can substitute for this continuous process. In fact, the process of teaming is so important that I encourage you to go on-line anytime at www.tompkinsinc.com/think and read Chapters 7 and 8 of **Revolution: Take Charge Strategies for Business Success.** These chapters discuss in-depth how you can transform an organization's culture through teams.*

There's no I in team, but there is in win.

Although organizations generally have teaming programs in place, most focus on using teams to win rather than promoting the process of teaming. The subliminal message is that teaming is in place for the sake of winning–hence the quote above, which is attributed to Michael Jordan.

Winners never quit and quitters never win.

Win with teamwork.

Win one for the Gipper.

Winners do what they need to do; losers do what they want to do.

Expect to win.

To be a winner, all you need is to give all you have.

If you snooze, you lose.

  The Most Trite, Generic, Hokey, Overused, Cliched or Unmotivating Motivational Slogans •

I can always tell when a company is in trouble when I begin to hear football jargon enter the management vocabulary. Although there are many examples, my absolute favorite (repeated too many times in this camp) is: 'Winning in the fourth quarter.' By choosing this trite phrase, management implies that workers can miraculously overcome poor performance in the preceding three quarters. Also, having been asked to 'Win one for the Gipper' on several occasions so that he could make his MBO bonus trip to Hawaii while I stayed at home, never sits well.   *-Judith*

You have to be in it to win it.

Let's get out there and play to win!

The trouble with being a good sport is that you have to lose to prove it.

The Most Trite, Generic, Hokey, Overused, Cliched or Unmotivating Motivational Slogans •

The deal is win-win.

Really means: We paid too much for this acquisition, half the employees are about to get laid off, and the customers are about to get significant price increases while we sort out the incompatible computer systems that will manage to lose their orders for six months to a year. Now, let's open that bottle of Dom.

-Bob

It's not whether you win or lose,
it's how you play the game.

This last slogan has been around for centuries, but in a lot of business and organizational situations, it still has merit. Winning may gain you short-term glory, but the next step is likely to be a loss. Continually improving your playing skills and your game plan will mean you play the game well and will achieve long-term glory and avoid the valleys of business. Again, you must think about continuous, continuous improvement to achieve Peak-to-Peak performance.

People are our greatest asset.

Teaming and winning aren't really possible without people. Organizations have various slogans on the subject.

[Insert company name here]: A place where people make the difference.

We are people oriented.

Can't we all just get along?

Companies don't succeed, people do.

Our most important ingredient is people.

Our people make the difference.

People are our business, our only business.

People don't buy from companies; people buy from people.

Treat employees like partners and they act like partners.

  The Most Trite, Generic, Hokey, Overused, Cliched or Unmotivating Motivational Slogans •

It is all very well to claim that people are your company's most important asset, but do you really treat them as if they are? Tired and unappreciated employees who aren't treated well don't believe these slogans, because they know the company is paying lip service to a trend in clever slogans while doing business as usual. Or, as another slogan submitted to the contest says, "The whip makes the mule pull the wagon with resentment." If you really want your company to succeed, you really need to think of your employees and their knowledge as assets on the company's balance sheet. If employees believe that you value them as partners, they will work with you to achieve ongoing success.

Chapter 7
When you can't change the wind, adjust the sail.

Dealing with Change

Change is often addressed in organizational slogans because, quite frankly, change is inevitable. Adjusting the sail addresses the opportunity to adapt to the situation at hand. The alternative, complaining about the wind, provides no progress. Our contestants sent in several slogans that advocate making adjustments.

A bend in the road is not the end of the road, unless you fail to make the turn.

It's time for a paradigm shift.

If you're not riding the wave of change...you'll find yourself beneath it.

If you don't have plans to drive events, then let events drive your plans.

Participation is the key to positive change.

Temporary inconvenience for permanent improvement.

People who manage change are influenced by people who manufacture change.

Manufacture positive change!

Although this last slogan has a positive message, the message is confused. First of all, you cannot manage change. In other words, managing change requires redirecting the wind. Good luck. Managing change is an oxymoron. To manage means to control. In today's dynamic environment, do you believe anyone has the ability ▶

to control change? The pace of change is increasing and the key to dealing with change is harnessing its energy. Many resist change because it often requires pain. People and companies need to understand that pain is not the challenge. How you respond to the pain is the challenge. Harness change, develop your organization's resilience to deal with its pain, and continually stay in partnerships with your customers throughout change. Want to know more about developing your own and your company's resilience? Go on-line to www.tompkinsinc.com/think. When you harness the energy of change, you can adjust the sail and use the energy to move in the right direction.

We're going to grow the business.

Aarrgh! You can grow corn, peas, and flowers, as well as more. You increase the amount of business! I find it most apropos that a certain bovine byproduct is a substantial part of organic life. It seems to exist in corporate life in abundance!   *-Dan*

> ## Perhaps the only person who likes change is a wet baby.
>
> This is a slogan from a presentation about our company's upcoming merger. It can be construed as a means of corporate brainwashing. Some can handle change better than others, so the content deals with the psychology of change. I presume some merger consultant company has provided this electronic psycho-babble stuff because it could be a cheaper alternative to hiring instructors to come in and offer the same material via courses.
>
> *-Name Withheld*

"IF IT AIN'T BROKE ..."

Among the worst things an organization and its employees can do is to resist change or ignore it. Unfortunately, many of the slogans we received suggested either or both.

The more things change, the more they stay the same.

Expect the best; prepare for the worst.

Here we grow again.

Just keep on keepin' on.

Keep on truckin'.

Been there, done that.

Let sleeping dogs lie.

Let's not reinvent the wheel.

Continuous improvement often means reinventing the wheel. You may not want to go all the way back to the drawing board, but there will always be a place in the process where continuous improvement is key to success.

THE FUTURE

As we've said, the future and change go hand in hand. Numerous slogans address the future.

The future lies ahead.

Live for today, but work toward tomorrow.

Looking to the future, remembering the past.

Make today count for tomorrow.

If it ain't broke, don't fix it.

This remains largely unchallenged and may explain the last phase of the product cycle.   *-Frank*

Let's not reinvent the wheel.

We use this all the time in our guidance office, because there is so much to do and the pace never slows down. So, we find ourselves always trying to save time.   *-Linda*

My interest is the future, because I'm going to spend the rest of my life there.

Yesterday is the last day of the past.

The future's so bright, I gotta wear shades.

The best way to predict the future is to create it.

It's a new era.

After a gruesome reorganization resulting in many talented people walking out the door, our organization posted this to reassure us that things would now be better. Judging from the low morale and chaos that followed, along with the employees' vote of 'no confidence,' this sign should have read: 'It's another error.'

–Name Withheld

"

Your future is bright with...

This was printed on a pair of cheap sunglasses and given to employees the same day the company announced a 'Workforce Resizing Program' aimed at eliminating 6,000 management jobs.

-Cristi

"

The Most Trite, Generic, Hokey, Overused, Cliched or Unmotivating Motivational Slogans •

In order to seize the future, you must grasp the present.

This last slogan has merit. In business, the past is not a good indicator of the future. Rather, the future is an extension of the present based upon the background of the past. If we are to meet today's challenges and create a vision of the future, we must act upon this understanding.

Chapter 8
Life's tough...get over it.
Employee Humor

Although I prefer to emphasize the positive, I could not help notic-ing the cynical tone in many slogans submitted to our contest. Most were "cubicle humor"-sayings posted in offices but not meant as serious slogans— at least I hope these entries were cubicle humor, not real company slogans.

A hundred years from now it won't matter.

Don't worry about tomorrow. You don't know if you will make it through today.

Good enough—never is!

I know the raise isn't large, but you have plenty of headroom.

This is used by most major corporations at employee review time.

-Larry

Hey, it beats a poke in the eye with a sharp stick!

I can only please one person per day, today is not your day, and tomorrow isn't looking good either.

After everything has been said and done, there is always more said than done.

As I slide down the banister of life, I'll remember you as a splinter in my butt.

Avoid viable alternatives like the plague!

"

Typical required management retreat for executives: 'In order to squeeze a 30-minute presentation into a three-day seminar, let's go to breakout sessions. After lunch, we'll do flipcharts.'

-Lynn

"

Cheer up. Things will get worse.

No good deed ever goes unpunished.

Do you want the man in charge or the woman who knows what is going on?

I may as well do something, even if it is wrong.

If it looks like I'm listening, you must be blind.

When you're up to your ass in alligators, it's hard to remember your initial objective was to drain the swamp.

Management told you it was a fish pond and you can bet their asses aren't in there with you.

-Jim

123

If you can't run with the big dogs, stay on the porch.

If you lie down with dogs, you're gonna get fleas.

People that believe that the dead never come back to life should be here at quitting time.

Raising standards by lowering expectations.

Shoot for the stars and settle for the moon.

"

The world applauds screwball clods.

"

It may be that your sole purpose in life is to serve as a warning to others.

It's strange how unimportant your job is when you're asking for a raise and how important it can be when you want the day off.

No one appreciates what you do unless what you do immediately benefits them.

It doesn't matter who's to blame (responsible), let's just fix it.

This slogan can be attributed to the various dictatorial, Machiavellian ogres I've worked for who will always find the some-one (usually the wrong person and certainly not themselves) to blame and nail for it. *—Bill*

You can't teach an old dog new tricks.
May be the basis for unabashed age-ism in the technology-driven workplace today. *-Frank*

  The Most Trite, Generic, Hokey, Overused, Cliched or Unmotivating Motivational Slogans •

How do you expect me to soar like an eagle when I work with a bunch of turkeys?

Referring to coworkers as turkeys is a self-centered approach. In reality, we are all accountable for making sure that everyone we work with soars like an eagle. Don't be negative about co-workers: build them up and make them strong. This negativity can also be seen in comments about life.

Life's a bitch and then you die.

Life is but a bitter interruption into an otherwise blissful nonexistence.

Life is like a pack of cigarettes—you never know what you get: lung cancer, high blood pressure, heart attack, etc.

Life is like a roll of toilet paper, the closer it gets to the end, the faster it goes.

Those who said it couldn't be done should not tell others how to do it.
Don't we all know a person who is a 'know-it-all' but doesn't like to work?   *-Maryann*

  131

"

Life's tough...get used to it.

"

Stating that life is tough is so negative when you can make life wonderful. Challenge the status quo to make real success and innovation a reality and never accept anything less than being wonderful. These next two "slogans" also seem especially shortsighted.

Now we do it MY way: plain and simple.

Rule #1: The boss is always right! Rule #2: When the boss is wrong, see Rule #1.

You've got a lemon. Now is your chance to make lemonade.

This was from the editor of the daily newspaper where I worked as city editor on the subject of a hopeless employee who should have been—and ultimately was—fired. My response—which was taken as an indication of a bad attitude—was that what I had was chicken manure and what I was being expected to make out of it was chicken salad!   -Tim

"My way is the only way" and "the boss is always right" are phrases that kill participation and continuous improvement. If the boss thinks he or she is right, then by definition, that boss is wrong. It is not about being right or wrong: it's about working together through continuous improvement to get better every day.

How do we deal with this negativism? We fall back on one of the biggest cliches of all:

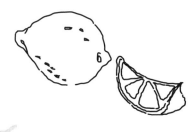

  135

When life gives you lemons, make lemonade.

Despite the fact that one of our contestants felt that making lemonade from lemons was trite and really meant making chicken salad from chicken manure, I still like its underlying theme: making something positive out of the negative. We learn by reflecting and by finding the positive possibilities in all situations. One only has to look at people who suffered severe physical setbacks such as Christopher Reeves' quadriplegic state to see what the human spirit can achieve by focusing on the possibilities. The same is true in every situation that we face. I believe we need to deal with reality and work toward making the best of every challenge placed before us. I truly believe that all things (and I mean ALL THINGS) occur for a reason and it is not our job to always understand why, but it is our job to be sure we learn and move forward with continuous, continuous improvement.

Chapter 9
The Last Word on Thinking Outside the Box

  139

As I stated in Chapter 1, "Think outside the box," means "Go beyond the limits of conventional wisdom to find solutions." But even when we think outside the box, we base our thinking on logic and intuition. Some people thought that thinking outside the box meant reacting to the slogans they found most trite and annoying and rewriting them. The most common examples of these rewrites were the "If at first you don't succeed..." slogans in Chapter 6. Enjoy some more.

Either fish or get stuck cutting bait.

Expect excellence; accept mediocrity.

For the good of the country, go back to bed!

Never do today what you can put off for tomorrow.

He who has the gold makes the rules.

In light of all the corporate mergers, downsizing, etc., it appears as though we are truly experiencing this paraphrase of the golden rule.

-Stan

Walk the talk—don't stumble the mumble.

The grass is always greener under the fence.

No goals, no glory.

No quote, no pay.

Uncertainty breeds inventory.

You can't spell dumb without U.

Some people who entered the slogan contest, however, thought entirely outside the box, or they ignored the box—I'm not sure which. Following is a smattering of offbeat quotations and catchphrases that range from the whimsical to the baffling.

Do not use a hatchet to remove a fly from a friend's forehead.

Although this is a colorful way of saying to use restraint, it is more of a quotable quote than a slogan. Lizzie Borden could have used this advice.

  145

Don't worry about the mule being poor. Just load the wagon.

I understand the thought behind these words: Don't become distracted. But whether I rely on a person, an animal, or a machine to complete a task, I need to know their limitations and take them into consideration.

Go ahead...Make my day.

The person who thought this was an overworked slogan must have a boss named Harry Callaghan (alias, Dirty Harry).

146

Drudgery is a fatiguing expenditure of energy.

In other words, dull, repetitive tasks exhaust us mentally and physically. However, the slogan itself is fatiguing, which I guess was the intent. Anyway, why not emphasize the positive? I prefer to say, "Challenging work refreshes us mentally even when it tires us physically." Even that kind of advice is less helpful than preparing everyone in an organization to harness the energy of change and integrate their efforts—thus making everyone's work more challenging and rewarding.

Ignorance is no excuse for the law.

I disagree. I could make a strong case that many bad laws get passed, and ignorance is the only possible excuse for many of them. The original saying, which means something entirely different, is, "Ignorance of the law excuses [no one]..." This statement is as true of the laws of economics as it is of legal issues. For example, an organization that is ignorant of the natural pattern of success, peak-to-valley, will be condemned to repeat that pattern until it learns how to address the problem and attain Peak-to-Peak.

In fact, all of the sayings we've looked at—whether genuine slogans or the strange mix of quotations in this chapter—are no substitute for a fundamental organizational revolution. As I mentioned in Chapter Two, designing a Model of Success (MOS) and aligning everyone in the organization with the MOS will lead to continuous, continuous improvement and Peak-to-Peak performance.

GO! GO! GO!

(I'll leave it up to my publisher to discuss this!)

Publisher's Note

Since I began to work for Jim Tompkins a number of years ago, every idea and every path forward is met with GO! GO! GO! It used to come on handwritten memos, then on voice mails, and finally, now on e-mails. It is Jim's way of encouraging, prodding, celebrating, and letting you know it is time to get on with it!

Over the years, we have mutated it on occasion—backwards it is Og! Og! Og! We have used it as a source of humor at a company retreat—where some inspired retreat team provided each participant with a notepad featuring Jim's picture and GO! GO! GO!—the men's room was papered with sheets of the notepad.

Occasionally, the reckless employee has asked for four

instead of three. But through all of this, we have understood the message and appreciated its consistency. The GO! GO! GO! is not here today and gone tomorrow. In a company that moves at the speed of e, it is an ever-constant message of encouragement and progress.

-Brenda Jernigan
Publisher

P.S. Tompkins Press, the leader in cutting edge business publications, invites you to visit us at www.tompkinsinc.com/think and enjoy more trite, generic, hokey, overused, cliched or unmotivating motivational slogans or submit your own for the **Slogan of the Day**. Had a motivational idea that worked? Enter our latest contest, **Thinking Outside the Box Contest: Employee Motivation Strategies That Work.**

About the Author

Jim Tompkins is the President and founder of Tompkins Associates. Jim is a prolific author and has written and contributed to more than 20 books. A dynamic and captivating speaker, Jim has presented more than 3,000 seminars, speeches, roundtables, and workshops to executive level audiences worldwide on a variety of business issues.

About Tompkins Associates

Tompkins Associates is the leader in Total Operations consulting, integration and implementation. With three decades of experience, Tompkins provides expertise in Material Handling Integration, Supply Chain Synthesis, warehousing, logistics, order fulfillment, manufacturing, systems implementation, construction services, organizational excellence, quality, and maintenance.

TOMPKINS
ASSOCIATES

Total Operations Consulting ■ Systems Implementation ■ Material Handling Integration

TOMPKINS

A S S O C I A T E S

Total Operations Excellence

CORPORATE HEADQUARTERS
2809 Millbrook Road
Raleigh, NC 27604
(800) 789-1257
FAX (919) 872-9666
www.tompkinsinc.com

OFFICE LOCATIONS
Allentown, Pennsylvania
Atlanta, Georgia
Buenos Aires, Argentina
Chicago, Illinois
Fountain Valley, California
Irving, Texas
Monterrey, Mexico
Orlando, Florida
Raleigh, North Carolina
The Netherlands
Toronto, Canada
Warwick, United Kingdom